Powerful Principles

for Choosing

a Marriage Partner

Powerful Principles for Choosing a Marriage Partner

Jesse L. McNeil
Family Pastor, Teacher and Advisor

BookSurge Publishing
Charleston, South Carolina

ISBN: 1-4392-6325-6
ISBN-13: 9781439263259

Jesse L. McNeil
Family Focus Ministry
email: ffm@tampabay.rr.com

This book is dedicated to

my lovely wife, Brenda, who

is my princess and my queen all in one.

Table of Contents

Foreword ....*ix*

Preface..*xiii*

Acknowledgements ....*xv*

Principle #1 Don't Be in a Hurry.........................*1*

Principle #2 Marry Someone Who Is Born Again and Loves

the Lord *9*

Principle #3 Does He Have a Vision?...............*15*

Principle #4 Look Beyond the Exterior *19*

Principle #5 Is He or She Selfish?....................*23*

Principle #6 How Does Your Partner Treat Others?............*27*

Principle #7 How Does Your Partner Manage Money?.......*31*

Principle #8 How Does Your Future Mate Handle Anger?...*37*

Principle #9 Does He Have a Job? Will He Work? Can He

Keep a Job?..*41*

Principle #10 Does He or She Want Children?.....................*45*

Principle #11 Does He or She Understand Submission?.....*51*

Principle #12 Before Getting Married, Plan to Attend

Premarital Preparation...*57*

Conclusion...69

The Prayer of Salvation...73

Future Spouse Confession..77

Ending an Unhealthy Relationship.................................81

Positive Qualities for a Great Relationship.....................85

About the Author..87

Recommended Resources..89

* * * **Foreword** * * *

In life, many people get the right answers to the wrong questions. Two of the most important questions in life are: Who will you marry? What local congregation will you covenant with in any given season of your life? The second question is designed to be carefully and prayerfully thought out based upon where you are, the needs of yourself and your family during a particular season, and of course, the leading of the Holy Spirit. However, the first question is ordained by God to be one that is asked and answered only once in a lifetime. Unfortunately, far too many, even Christians, put substantially more energy, research, and resources into answering the question of planning the wedding day than in planning the life of marriage.

I, along with my wife Linda, have been privileged to work with thousands of couples on five continents. We have discovered that being in too much of a hurry to get married and failing to invest quality time and resources into research are the root causes of the failure of so many marriages.

What God said to Jeremiah about nations is just as applicable to marriage: *"See, I have appointed you this day over the nations and over the kingdoms, to pluck up and to break down, to destroy and to overthrow, to build and to plant."*

In marriage preparation, God's word to Jeremiah speaks to a process that must be walked through to ensure that you have, to the best of your ability, identified things in yourself, things in your potential mate, and things in one another's family of origin so that you know what type of foundation on which you're building. One of my favorite quotes outside of the Word of God is by Dr. Ron Jensen, who states, "Society reflects the health of institutions, which reflect the health of families, which reflect the health of individuals." Therefore, we can bring radical restoration and transformation to communities, cities, and the institutions within them with a determined effort toward marriage preparation and education.

My covenant friends, Pastors Jesse and Brenda McNeil, have walked out the principles and pattern that they present in this simple yet profound book on fulfillment in marriage by finding the right mate. The Word of God declares that you will "*... know a tree by its fruit*"; however, the quality and condition of the fruit is always determined by the root!

In this book, Pastor Jesse has provided the root principles that create the cornerstone of healthy marriage and family fruit. The family is the foundation of any institution or society; therefore, nations and the world can be transformed through truth-filled marriage relationship education. I encourage every person who picks up this book to not just read it, but to prayerfully practice the principles in your pursuit of a marriage mate and become a part of a marriage and family revolution.

R. Earl Brown, Ph.D, DMin, Senior Pastor and International

Marriage/Relationship Coach and Coach Trainer

* * * **Preface** * * *

The question is, "Will this marriage last?" Genesis 2:24 says, *"therefore shall a man leave his father and his mother and shall cleave to his wife and the two shall be one flesh."* Think about this. At the time of a couple's wedding there are factors already present that can raise the odds of divorce to as high as 70–75% or lower it to nearly 20–25%. Couples who have attended premarital preparation cut their odds of divorce by almost one third. Research has shown that couples who have gone through premarital preparation have less hurtful conflicts and higher marital satisfaction. Premarital preparation might be the best wedding gift any newlyweds can receive.

There are only three reasons for meeting people: (1) for a specific reason, (2) for a season, (3) for a lifetime. According to scripture, marriage should be forever (Matthew 19:6). So let us get it right the first time so it will last for a lifetime.

* * * **Acknowledgements** * * *

First, I give special thanks to the Lord Jesus Christ for His goodness and mercy, which are always with me. To my wife, Brenda (Bren), thank you for being my powerful prayer partner, my spiritual growth partner, and for your timeless hours of support and teamwork. You are amazing!

Special thanks to my children, Monya, Myron, and Vontrece, for being patient with me as I have endeavored to become a father of understanding. I love you all very much. Thanks to my grandchildren, Yazmine, R.J., Teke, and Mariah for being who you are; you are so precious. To my mother, Charlotte and my mother-in-law Clementine, you have inspired me with your history of perseverance.

Much family love to my brothers, C.D., Doward, William, and Jerome, and my sisters, Annie and Rena.

To my brother-in-law, Rev. D.A. Lattimore, Jr., pastor of Mount Ararat M.B. Church, Jacksonville, Florida, thank you for being a pioneer of the gospel and for portraying much spiritual endurance over your many years in ministry.

To my pastor, Edgar Pickett III of Word Alive Ministries, Inc., Lakeland, Florida, thanks for your spiritual growth teachings and your constructive and motivating messages, which have inspired me to continue in developing my spiritual muscles with each new day.

To Mr. Phillip Walker, Allstate agent in Lakeland, Florida, thank you for your positive and inspiring drive in the area of leadership.

To Mr. Anthony Broadnax, electrical engineering technician of Lakeland Electric, Lakeland, Florida, thank you for being a person of such compassion and understanding.

To Ezra and Camilla Gittens, thank you for always extending to me your kindness and hospitality.

To Bill and Sharon Gray, thank you for being excited about God's idea for a good marriage.

To Justin and Donna Daley, and Ralph and Diana Gibbs, thank you for being true friends to the end.

To Ms. Angie Lisbon, a dear friend, thank you for your special ability to bring laughter to every situation.

I give special recognition to Pastor Walter K. Laidler and his wife Carrie, of Christ Community Christian Center Church, Lakeland, Florida, for their orderly image and blamelessness.

I would like to thank the following pastors for the many seeds they have sown into my life: Pastor Earl Brown of Freely Forgiven Community Church in Lakeland, Florida; Pastor Harry Riley of Lakewin Christian Center in Riverdale, Georgia and Pastor Reginald Ezell of World Covenant Church in Stockbridge, Georgia (ministry sons of Pastor Creflo Dollar of Atlanta, Georgia); Dr. Clyde Narramore, Christian psychologist, of Rosemead, California; and Pastor Robert Schuller of Garden Grove, California.

To the late Pastor Edward Lewis, former pastor of Macedonia P.B. Church, Lakeland, Florida, thank you for the performance of your first wedding ceremony, which united my wife and me in holy matrimony many, many years ago.

To all who have deposited into my life the good, the clean, the pure, the powerful, and the positive seeds concerning marriage, family, and ministry, I would like to say, thank you

so much. May God bless you, keep you, and may the favor of

God surround you like a shield. You are very special.

Beware of the urge to merge.

Get to know their

Past Personal Profile.

Play Investigative Journalist.

Principle #1

Don't Be in a Hurry

*N*ever be in a hurry to get married. Appropriate waiting power is necessary. Before establishing a marriage covenant, it is wise to establish a waiting covenant. The Father God tells us in Philippians 4:6, *"Be anxious for nothing, but in everything by prayer and supplication with thanksgiving let your request be made known unto God."* Beware of the "urge to merge." Always look before you leap. The "get to know" process takes time. It is your opportunity to lovingly and graciously gather information on a person's character. Sometimes you have to play investigative journalist and check out things like background, family, values, career, lifestyle, habits, and financial obligations. Keep in mind that when you first meet someone, you meet personality, not character. Allow time to be your friend.

By no means get married in a short span of time. Many Jewish families were set on a one-year waiting covenant before

It is dangerous to

rush into the unknown.

Know what you want

in a mate and stick

to it. Allow time

to be your friend.

their daughters were given in marriage. Do not push the process or overlook important red flags because you are lonely, under pressure from relatives and friends, or reaching a certain age. Proverbs 19:2 says, *"Desire without knowledge is not good and to be overhasty is to sin and miss the mark"* (AMP). The Living Bible says, *"It is dangerous and sinful to rush into the unknown."*

If you are a believer, I say to you, get involved in the different areas of ministry in your local church. Be active in the church and continue hearing the Word of God for spiritual strength, spiritual guidance and spiritual development. Psalms 92:13 says, *"Those that are planted in the house of the Lord shall flourish in the courts of our God."* Plant yourself in a local church and allow faith muscles to develop, because *"faith comes by hearing and hearing by the Word of God"* (Romans 10:17).

Let me share some scriptures with you concerning spiritual guidance. The scripture in Isaiah 40:31 says, *"They that wait on the Lord shall renew their strength; they shall*

Don't be impulsive,

Don't be impetuous.

Beware of your past

mistakes and don't

repeat them.

mount up with wings as eagles; they shall run and not be weary, and they shall walk and not faint." Now let's go back to the beginning of that scripture. They that wait on the Lord shall renew their strength or shall be refreshed with wisdom to spot any hidden works of darkness during the dating process. They shall be on top of their situation, full of vitality and ready for action.

The Word of God tells us to walk circumspectly, not as fools, but as wise men (Ephesians 5:15, KJV). The word *circumspectly* means to pay attention to the things that surround you. There may be something you need to know about your significant other that he/she is not telling you. For example, is he or she divorced? Is the divorce final? What is his/her credit score? And much, much more. We must trust God for wisdom to reveal any hidden works of darkness.

Psalms 27:14 says, *"Wait on the Lord, be of good courage and He shall strengthen your heart"* (KJV). He will strengthen your heart with what? Once again, He will strengthen your heart with wisdom. He said to wait, so don't be

He will instruct you

and teach you the

way you should go.

He is Jehovah-Rohi

"A Shepherd God"

for His people.

impulsive and don't be impetuous. Wait, I say on the Lord. If you are not a believer, I say to you, give your life to Christ.

John 1:12 says, *"But as many as received him, to them gave he power to become the sons/daughters of God, even to them that believe on his name."* Make Him Lord over your life and over your affairs.

Psalms 32:8 says, *"I [the Lord] will instruct you and teach you in the way you should go. I will counsel you with My eye upon you"* (AMP). Now He is going to instruct, teach and guide only those who believe, so believe and receive Him today. (Salvation instructions are located in the rear of this book.)

Studies have found that

people with common

lifestyles and interests have

healthier and happier marriages.

Principle #2

Marry Someone Who Is
Born Again and Loves the Lord

*T*his principle is primarily the most important of all. If you and your future marriage partner are born again, you have become spiritually connected with God. Man is a spirit, he has a soul, and he lives in a body. Now listen to me closely. It is very important to understand the following statement: *Unless you get the spirit part of you right first, you will never be able to fix the other parts of you that are wrong.*

Before you get married, make sure the person you intend to marry is saved and committed to the Lord. I am not talking about a churchgoer, but I am talking about someone who has confessed Christ as his/her Savior and Lord. Your future marriage partner should be someone who has a practiced lifestyle of obedience and one who is excelling in sanctification.

Consider this scripture very carefully. II Corinthians 6:14 says, *"Be ye not unequally yoked together with*

Rebellion always brings serious consequences.

unbelievers, for what fellowship hath righteousness with un-righteousness and what communion hath light with dark-ness"* (KJV). Ask yourself, what kind of conversations will we have in common? If you get married, what kind of good, wholesome, and positive activities will you be able to enjoy together? Studies have found that people with simi-lar interests have happier marriages than those with differ-ent interests. Here are some more questions to ask yourself:

(1) How long has this person been a Christian?

(2) Is he/she active in the local church?

(3) Does he/she have a prayer life?

(4) Does this person make choices based on what God wants or based mainly on his/her own wants and desires?

(5) Does he/she apologize for misbehavior?

(6) When this person makes promises, does he/she always keep them or does he/she make excuses?

(7) Has this person filed bankruptcy or is he/she in debt? If so, why? How much in debt is he/she?

(8) Have you met his/her friends? What are they like?

(9) How does he/she drive? With courtesy? With hostility? Does he/she take chances or risk other people's lives?

(10) Does this person have a criminal record?

According to scripture, believers should marry believers. Two cannot walk together if they do not agree.

My friend, do not be like Samson in Judges, chapter 14. His parents tried to warn him about marrying someone who did not love the Lord. However, Samson in his rebellion said, "I want her, get her for me." Judges 14:1–3 reads, *"And Samson went down to Timnah and saw a woman in Timnah of the daughters of the Philistines. And he went up and told his father and mother, saying, I have seen a woman in Timnah of the daughters of the Philistines. Now therefore, get her for me as a wife. Then his father and mother said to him, Is there no woman among the daughters of your brethren, or among all my people, that you must go and get a wife from the uncircumcised Philistines? And Samson said to his father, get her for me, for she pleases me well"* (KJV). Now this was a sign of rebellion that ultimately brought serious consequences (According to scripture, believers should marry believers). Amos 3:3 will put more light on this matter: *"Can two walk together except they be agreed?"*

Get a vision, write it

down, and stay focused.

Have appropriate faith and

patience. Though it tarries,

wait for it because it

will surely come.

Principle #3

Does He Have a Vision?

A vision is a plan or a positive life mission for you and your future mate's life. You may be in the process of choosing a future mate; however, you need to know his vision. You need to ask, "Where are you taking me? Where are we going in life?"

Proverbs 29:18a reads, *"Where there is no vision, the people perish"* (KJV). Now let's read it this way: Where there is no vision, the family has no direction of where it is going. It is very important to have a vision and write that vision down to stay focused. One of my visions was to have not just a good marriage, but a great marriage. So I invested many years into educating and training myself to be disciplined enough to do whatever it took to fulfill my vision.

According to the Bible, the husband is the major visionary for his family. It is okay for the wife to have a vision; however, her vision should always work in unity with the husband's vision. It should never bring about division, strife or

God has created the

husband to be the visionary

for his family. If a husband

does not have a vision,

he should seek God for

purpose and direction.

(Proverbs 3:6)

confusion. It is the husband's responsibility to provide for the needs of his family; therefore, it is extremely important for the husband to have a clear plan about his family's future. For example, a husband's vision might be to someday own his own business so he can be in a better financial position to take care of his wife and children. This may require further preparation, such as going back to school to develop skills relating to his business. If a husband has a thought-out plan for the future of his family, then he is more likely to pursue the goals which he has set.

On the contrary, a husband who does not have a vision for his family may live from day to day and accept life as it is. He may never strive to achieve higher goals or to better the quality of life for himself or his family.

In Habakkuk 2: 2–3, it reads, *"Write the vision and make it plain on tables that he may run who reads it. For the vision is yet for an appointed time; but at the end it will speak, and it will not lie. Though it tarries, wait for it; because it will surely come, it will not tarry"* (KJV).

All that glitters is not gold.

Look for inner values and

inner qualities. Looking

only for faces and figures

can be deceptive.

Principle #4

Look Beyond the Exterior

*R*emember, "all that glitters is not gold." If you are a young lady looking to God for a mate, look beyond the three Ts—Tall, Tan, and Terrific. If you are a young man believing God for a mate, look beyond the fact that she might be a "Brick House," or stacked to perfection, 36–24–36.

If you want a spiritually inclined person to notice you, you should dress modestly, regardless of what the fashion world may dictate. Adorning yourself in appropriate dress, with modesty and soundness of mind, will make you more attractive to a godly person. Physical attraction is not a bad thing; however, never allow it to be the absolute thing. Looking only for faces and figures can be deceptive. Looks are just the wrapping on the package that will change with time. I Samuel 16:7 says, *"For the Lord seeth not as man; for man looketh on the outward appearance, but the Lord looketh on the heart"* (KJV).

Physical attraction is not a bad thing; however, never allow it to be the absolute thing. Look beyond the three Ts—<u>Tall</u>, <u>Tan</u> and <u>Terrific</u> and the BH, <u>Brick House</u>, stacked to perfection.

Look for inner values and inner qualities such as someone who is tenderhearted, humble, compassionate, courteous, and someone who has integrity and is sensitive to your needs. I Peter 3:4 gives us highlights on this matter. It reads, *"Let it be the inner adorning and beauty of the hidden person of the heart with incorruptible and unfading charm of a gentle and peaceful spirit, which is not anxious but is very precious in the sight of God"* (AMP).

In addition to looking beyond the exterior, you must also look beyond the idea of being sexually active. Sex before marriage is wrong and sinful. It opens the door to STD's, HIV, unplanned pregnancies, and emotional stress. Read I Corinthians 6:17-18. The following keys will help you to remain chaste while you wait for your future marriage partner:

(1) Stay busy doing the work of the Lord – Staying active spiritually and physically will help you to keep your God-given sex drive under control (Luke 2:49, Psalms 92:13).

(2) Reside Daily in His presence - For personal prayer life empowerment (II Chronicles 7:14, Mark 1:35).

(3) Continue to hear and practice the Word of God – To develop faith muscles (Romans 1:17, Romans 10: 17).

(4) Train and tame your thought life – To stay focused and keep your mind from wandering (II Corinthians 10:5, Philippians 4:8).

Never go into a relationship

thinking of what you can

get out of it, but rather,

what you can give, because

marriage is totally unselfish.

Principle #5

Is He or She Selfish?

*S*elfishness is the act of being stingy or self-centered. Many couples enter into marriage with the wrong concept, thinking, *What can this person do for me, instead of what can I do for this person.* Never go into a relationship thinking of what you can get out of it, but rather, go into a relationship thinking of what you can give. Marriage is totally unselfish. My wife shares these words constantly as we spiritually advise many young couples.

One must operate in the principle of sowing and reaping in order for the relationship to prosper. Galatians 6:8b says, *"He that soweth to the Spirit shall reap the things that pertain to life."* Or if you sow into your marriage, you shall reap the things that pertain to a good married life. Remember, give whatever your need is and you will reap the need met. For example, if you desire affection, then give affection in your relationship. Or if you desire respect from your mate, then give

God has promised when you sow, you reap what you sow, you reap greater than you sow, and you reap later than you sow (Galatians 6:7).

your mate respect. In other words, "what you sow is what you grow," because everything reproduces after its own kind (Genesis 1). Philippians 2:20–21 reads, *"For I have no man likeminded, who will naturally care for your state. For all seek their own, not the things which are Jesus Christ's."* Being concerned for the interest of Jesus Christ means we are selflessly concerned for the welfare of others, especially our mate. You may have heard that marriage is 50/50, but I submit to you that marriage is not 50/50 as you may have heard, but 100/100. See the spiritual equation for marriage below.

100%	+	100%	=	100%
1.00	+	1.00	=	1.00
		2	=	1
Husband	&	Wife	Are	One

"Therefore shall a man leave his father and his mother and shall cleave unto his wife, and they shall be one flesh"
(Genesis 2:24).

In the nature of life,

a mother always knows

the basic temperament

of her son. How your future

spouse treats his mother is

an indication of how

he may treat you.

Principle #6

How Does Your Partner Treat Others?

*D*o you constantly hear your partner putting down others, criticizing or making fun of them? If your partner is saying negative things to other people, then it is just a matter of time before he or she begins to say negative things to you. Look at it this way. Proverbs 18:21 says: *"Death and life are in the power of the tongue, and they that love it shall eat the fruit thereof."* The fruit this scripture speaks of refers to the residue or the outcome of the words which are spoken. Are they hurtful or helpful? Do they build up? Do they edify? Or do they belittle and devour? Let us also observe two additional scriptures concerning the way we speak. Proverbs 25:11 says, *"A word fitly spoken is like apples of gold in pictures of silver."* Ephesians 4:29 paints a beautiful picture of this principle. It says, *"Let no foul or polluting language, nor evil word nor unwholesome or worthless talk [ever] come out of your mouth, but only such [speech] as is good and beneficial to the spiritual*

Before offering your heart

to someone, pay attention to

his or her actions and observe

how your partner treats others.

progress of others, as is fitting to the need and the occasion, that it may be a blessing and give grace (God's favor) to those who hear it" (AMP).

If you are a woman who has an interest in a man and want to know what he's really like, don't ask his father or his brother, but talk to his sister or his mother. The Bible says it's unnatural for a mother to forget the baby she has nursed (Isaiah 49:15). As a general rule, a mother can really identify the basic nature of her son. How your future mate treats his mother is an indication of how he may treat you.

Before offering your heart to someone, pay attention to his or her actions and how they speak. Observe how your partner treats others. Let me suggest going out in groups and getting to know his or her family. This can be very helpful because group settings allow you to observe without being under a lot of pressure.

Financial stress in a relationship

is one of the major causes

of divorce, so proper money

management skills for the

relationship is imperative.

Principle #7

How Does Your Partner Manage Money?

*I*s your partner a wise spender? Does your partner exercise temperance with money? Are you aware of how your partner manages money? Matthew 25:14–30 gives us a very fundamental example of money management. It is referring to the parable of the talents. Talents are large amounts of money that one man gave or invested for increase. In verse 15, he gave five talents to one, to another he gave two, and to another he gave one. Straightway he took his journey.

The man with five talents (in a modern way of saying it) made investments in the bank for increase. Likewise, the man with two talents made investments for increase. However, the man with one talent had a selfish attitude, so he buried it and kept it to himself. Notice verses 24 and 26; he did not sow it, he did not save it, and he did not invest it. Jesus called him a slothful and lazy servant. I believe the application of this is that some people know, understand, and operate the law of increase

People are not born knowing how to manage money wisely; it is a learned behavior.

as they budget and manage their money properly, while others remain idle. They never sow, never save, never invest and therefore experience poverty. So, proper money management skills for the relationship are imperative. Financial stress in a relationship is one of the major causes of divorce. If you or your partner is experiencing financial difficulty due to mismanagement of money or indebtedness, I would suggest that you seek some type of financial advice from your local church or a trained professional.

Let's talk about money personalities. There are five main money personalities. Each of these personalities has strengths and weaknesses, with the need for temperance. Let me explain.

(1) <u>The Spenders</u> can be generous with gifts on self or the people they love; however, unmanaged spending can lead to much debt.

(2) <u>The Savers</u> generally have little debt challenges, but can be labeled as cheapskates or tightfisted.

It is extremely important to maintain balance and trust God for wisdom and money moderation in handling finances.

(3) <u>The Security Seekers</u> are great planners and know how to use money to build a financial future, but they can be short-sighted and put off living for today.

(4) <u>The Risk Takers</u> are always looking for a money-making adventure; nevertheless, if they are not careful, may end up broke or bankrupt.

(5) <u>The Flyers</u> are usually free from stress about money and passionate about life and relationships, but can be headed for big financial trouble because often they give less attention to things like bills, over-draft fees, over-the-limit notices and late fees.

In which of the above categories are you and your future mate? There are pros and cons to each money personality, therefore, it is extremely important to maintain balance and trust God for wisdom and money moderation in handling finances. How you manage your money personality is very important for a fruitful relationship.

Which CUP best

describes your future

marriage partner?

Is he or she

Cool Under Pressure,

or does he or she

Curse Under Pressure?

Principle #8

How Does Your Future Mate Handle Anger?

*W*hen the pressures of life appear, how does your mate handle the situation? The Bible says in Ephesians 4:26, *"Be ye angry and sin not: let not the sun go down on your wrath"*. This means we should resolve disputes quickly. God desires for us to reconcile a matter within twenty-four hours. It's not a sin to be angry, but it's what we say and do when we become angry that may result in sin.

Does your mate respond to situations or does your mate react to them? Responding is positive, when we act in a way that is edifying and causes no regrets. Reacting can be negative, when it involves fulfilling our fleshly and sinful desires by doing the first thing that comes into our minds. Reacting negatively results in feelings of disappointment or even shame. Ecclesiastes 7:9 reads, *"Do not hasten [or be quick] in your spirit to be angry, for anger [uncontrolled anger] rests in the bosom of fools"* (NKJV).

Confess your faults one

to another to bring

about restoration,

reconciliation and

healing. We must

trust God to reveal any

hidden works of darkness.

Let's look at Nehemiah 5:6–7a, *"And I was very angry when I heard their cry and these words and I consulted with myself...."* He hit the pause button (*Selah*). Pray and think before you approach the matter. Now let me say this; if you are angry and in conflict with someone, you are to go to that person, in love, to resolve the situation (Matthew 5:23–24, Matthew 18:13). Jesus tells us to go to the individual and express your hurts and concerns. Let the healing flow, and then come to me with your gifts and worship. In addition, we read in James 5:16, *"Confess your faults one to another,"* which means we sit down and talk with dialogue and empathy so that healing and comfort can be restored. Remember that we were all given the ministry of reconciliation, regardless of who was at fault. II Corinthians 5:18 says, *"And all things are of God, who has reconciled us to Himself by Jesus Christ, and has given to us the ministry of reconciliation."*

Ladies, make sure your partner

has a job, will work, and

will keep a job.

Principle #9

Does He Have a Job?

Will He Work? Can He Keep a Job?

*T*he Father God declares, *"Because of laziness, the building decays, and through idleness of the hands, the house leaks"* (Ecclesiastes 10:18 NKJV). All forms of laziness bring houses and lives into disrepair. Ladies should be very mindful of choosing a mate who will work and one who can keep a job.

Think about this. Before God gave man a wife, he gave him a job. His job was to manage the garden. Adam was a steward in the Garden of Eden. A steward is a manager or overseer of something that belongs to someone else. In Genesis 2:15, it states, *"And the Lord God took the man and put him in the Garden of Eden to dress it and to keep it."* In other words, Adam was a cultivator. A cultivator is someone who produces something fruitful or someone who promotes or improves the growth of (plants, crops, lives, etc.) by labor, attention and oversight.

A very familiar quote is,

"Love will give you a thrill,

but it will not pay your bills."

A man's responsibility is to guide, decide, and provide for his family. Make sure your partner is someone who is able to provide for you and have the best interest of your future family at heart. Furthermore, make sure you know his outlook on life. Is he ambitious, and does he have any constructive goals? A very familiar quote is, "Love will give you a thrill, but it will not pay your bills."

The significance about work is that it exposes the man's potentials. A man cannot show what he is made of unless demands are placed upon him, and those demands are placed upon him by work. In Genesis 2:2a, we see that God himself worked during creation. *"And on the seventh day God ended his work which He had made;"* And God is still at work to carry out His divine purpose. *"For it is God which worketh in you both to will and to do of His good pleasure"* (Philippians 2:13).

Remember this my covenant friend. If your future marriage partner has a history of laziness and idleness of hands, he may not be a productive marriage mate.

God has graced the woman

to bring forth fruit in

her womb in order for

Him to have a godly seed.

He calls children a blessing.

Principle #10

Does He or She Want Children?

*A*t the beginning of a relationship, I would suggest not talking about whether or not your mate wants to have children. However, this should be addressed as the relationship progresses. Find out before marriage if he or she wants children or if he or she likes children. This subject should be given much thought, because it is not wise to get into a serious relationship without knowing where the other stands on this matter. Read with me in Psalms 127:3, which says, *"Children are a heritage of the Lord and the fruit of the womb is his reward."*

A heritage is something handed down or given to generations as a custom. Good and godly parents would pass on their love and faith to their children for stability in life; so our God has graced the woman to bring forth fruit in her womb in order for Him to have a godly seed (Malachi 2:15). God calls children a blessing (Deuteronomy 7:13). I know that sometimes we as parents go through some challenging times to bring up

If children are already present in the relationship, observe your future partner's actions, attitudes, and verbal tones toward them.

our children in the nurture and admonition of the Lord (Ephesians 6:4). Nurture and admonition means showing love while at times giving constructive discipline. I understand that, because I am a parent myself. My wife and I had to press, push, and persevere in prayer, with patience, in raising our children. Nevertheless, when they are grown and gone (Proverbs 22:6), you can look back and say, "Hallelujah, with the Lord's help, we did it!" Now they are able to start their own families.

Then come grandchildren, calling you Mema and Oompa, or whatever! That is why it is very important to know how your future spouse feels about children. It will help to eliminate problems later, after the marriage is final. Find out clearly and precisely how your partner feels about having children. Is it yea or nay? If it is yea (yes), how many and when? If it is nay (no), what seems to be the problem? Be sure that your partner explains. You want no mishaps and no surprises.

If children are already present in the relationship, observe actions, attitudes and verbal tones toward them.

"The soul that is without knowledge is not good" (Proverbs 19:2a).

Let me add this; if there are older children involved, get some feedback from them about how they view your future mate. You may ask them something like, "What do you think about this man or woman as my future mate?" Knowing how the children feel will help you to bring about harmony and resolve any conflict between your children and your future mate as the need arises.

My final thoughts on this matter are reflected in Proverbs 19:2a, *"The soul that is without knowledge is not good."* Putting it differently, the more information you gather, the wiser you will be. It is very, very helpful to know what your future marriage partner thinks about children.

Harmony, synergy, and positive

energy are imperative for the

growth of any relationship.

Spiritual teamwork effort

always glorifies God.

Principle #11

Does He or She Understand Submission?

*T*he Bible is very clear about submission in regards to relationships. *Sub* means to come under. Otherwise stated, submission is to willfully come under the mission, to come under the plan, or to come under the vision of someone else. The Bible talks about how the male-man is to come under God's dominion assignment, which is the will of God on the earth for success and prosperity.

In a marriage, a wife would be wise to come under her husband's God-given mission. She should support, encourage and exhibit a teamwork effort within the relationship, because two are better than one (Ecclesiastes 4:9). Consider these scriptures in terms of rank, order, and synergy. I Corinthians 11:3 says, *"But I would have you to know that the head of every man is Christ, and the head of the woman is the man, and the head of Christ is God."* I Corinthians 11:9 says the woman was made for whatever the man has; all his vision, all his hopes, all

The woman was made for what the man has; all his vision, all his hopes, and all his dreams. She was made to help bring them to pass. He cannot accomplish them without her precious support.

his dreams. She was made to help bring them to pass. Also in I Corinthians 11:11, it states, *"Neither is the man without the woman, neither the woman without the man in the Lord."* As you get to know another person, you must understand your God-given place and position in the relationship while you move forward to glorify God.

Let us talk a little more about submission. Submission is three-fold, which I will refer to as MSP—mutual, spiritual and positional. In Eph. 5:21–23 you will find these three types of submission. In verse 21, Paul refers to mutual submission or submission to each other, *"submitting yourselves one to another in the fear of God."* In verse 22, Paul talks about spiritual submission. This type of submission is about principle not preference. We are to submit as it is fit in the Lord; *"Wives, submit yourselves unto your own husbands as unto the Lord."*

A wife should submit as long as it is not illegal, immoral, or unethical. In verse 23, the apostle Paul elaborates on positional submission, which deals with rank or order, *"For the husband*

God tells husbands to love

their wives as Christ

loves the Church,

not rule them.

is the head of the wife, even as Christ is the head of the church, and he is the savior of the body."

Only the carnal man or woman rebels when it comes to submission; however, the spirit-filled man or woman usually has no problem in any area of submission. Submission in marriage is not a master to slave relationship, as some may think of it. In Ephesians 5:25, God tells husbands to love their wives (not rule them), even as Christ loves the church. A husband's love for his wife should never be a domineering or controlling love. It should be a love that is unselfish, caring, adoring, thoughtful, and giving. This is the kind of love that God desires for a husband to demonstrate towards his wife.

My friend, there is so much blessing in submission. Submission is a matter of the heart. It is about first, submitting your heart to the will of God, then following up with your actions. Treasure these words in your heart, *"If you are willing and obedient, you shall eat the good of the land"* (Isaiah 1:19).

Research has shown that couples

who receive premarital

preparation have less hurtful

conflicts than couples who

do not prepare themselves

before marriage.

Principle #12

Before Getting Married, Plan to Attend

Premarital Preparation

*A*ttending premarital preparation sessions from a spiritual advisor or Christian counselor before getting married will be one of the best investments you can make for your marriage. My wife and I have been blessed to teach and empower couples on how to have successful relationships. Our advisory is based on godly principles from the Word of God and from personal knowledge we have gained through many years of marriage. We offer six or more powerful sessions.

Research has shown that couples who receive premarital preparation have less hurtful conflicts, more love and understanding, more marital satisfaction, and a lower divorce rate than couples who do not prepare themselves before marriage.

Some counties strongly recommend that couples seek some type of premarital preparation before getting married and

God desires

for marriage

to be forever.

offer incentives such as discounts on marriage license fees and waiving the waiting period before receiving a marriage license. They suggest that couples receive advice in some of the major areas in which marriages have problems, such as conflict management, communication skills, financial responsibilities, and parenting.

Here is a brief description of how God has led us in conducting our premarital preparation sessions. Each week we are open to the leading of the Holy Spirit as to what each couple's needs are.

In the first session, the couple is asked to fill out a questionnaire that gathers general information about the couple. This questionnaire also prompts them to think about many important areas in marriage which they may need to address. After completion of the questionnaire, we review it with the couple and pay special attention to any areas of concern. These concerns are dealt with on a spiritual as well as practical level.

One major area covered on the questionnaire is, "Agreement on Economic Matters." Studies show that couples

Selfishness is one of the major reasons why people do not get along.

fight about money more than anything else. Also in a similar study, we found that seventy percent of divorced couples stated that money problems were one of the main causes of their divorce. For this reason, proper money management is vitally important for the success of a marriage.

Our second session is called, "A Biblical View of a Healthy Marriage." God desires for marriage to be forever. We give the couple a practical, clear, and Biblical viewpoint of marriage. This session expounds on the reasons for which a man and a woman were created, and helps them to understand their God-given purpose and design. We consider this session to be vital, for if we can understand what God did when he created us, it will eliminate an enormous amount of hurt, abuse, and misunderstanding, and bring about much enlightenment, companionship, and peace within marriage.

Session three covers "How to Handle Conflict." The objective of this session is to empower the couple when they are facing opposition and dealing with life's challenges. Selfishness is one of the major reasons why people do not get along, and it

Effective communication contributes to a healthy and lasting relationship.

causes much conflict. As we share about the undesirable consequences of selfishness, couples begin to see the destructive
affects it can have in a relationship. We conclude this session
by exploring five ways that people handle conflict, and direct
them toward the ideal way: the Biblical way, which we encourage them to adopt.

Communication is the gift of oneself. It is being physically
and emotionally present. In session four, we teach "Effective
Communication." The objective of this session is to help the
couple to talk, share, and listen to each other on a daily basis;
to make dialog and empathy a marital goal. We often share
Proverbs 25:11, *"Words fitly spoken are like apples of gold in
pictures of silver."* Effective communication contributes to a
healthy and lasting relationship.

Because money plays such an important role in marriage,
we found it necessary to include a financial segment in the
premarital preparation sessions. The fifth session is called
"Following God's Financial Plan." This session is designed to
help couples learn how to properly budget and manage their

Prayer is not an option,

it is a command.

Prayer is the key to

a lasting relationship.

finances through practical and biblical instructions. This will help them to operate in the law of increase in their marriage and also help to eliminate financial stress.

There is no way to express the extreme importance of prayer in a relationship and what praying together will do to enhance a marriage. We know that prayer is not an option, it is a command. Our final session is called, "Prayer—The Key to a Lasting Relationship." We discuss with the couple why we should pray and the benefits of prayer in our daily lives. When the couple understands the importance of prayer, we give them written prayer guides to help them develop a daily prayer schedule.

One important prayer guide we share with them is based on the Lord's Prayer, which is broken down into sections. The first section, *"Our Father which art in heaven,"* is where God presides. We know His holy habitation is in heaven; however, as born again believers, His Spirit abides within us. The second section, *"Hallowed be thy name,"* describes God's persons. The

The Acts Formula

A – Adoration

C – Confession

T – Thanksgiving

S – Supplication

third section, *"Thy kingdom come, thy will be done, on earth as it is in heaven,"* speaks of <u>God's</u> <u>plan</u> for us. The fourth section, *"Give us this day our daily bread,"* speaks of <u>God's</u> <u>provisions</u> for us. The fifth section, *"Forgive us our debts as we forgive our debtors,"* speaks of <u>God's</u> <u>pardon</u> in our lives. The sixth section, *"And lead us not into temptation, but deliver us from evil,"* speaks of <u>God's</u> <u>protection</u> over us. The seventh and last section is, *"For thine is the kingdom, and the power, and the glory, forever."*

We also share with the couple The Acts Formula: A—Adoration, C—Confession, T—Thanksgiving, and S—Supplication. This formula can help to guide them in their personal prayer time. These prayers are given to get the couple started as they build and expand in their spiritual growth. We are able to share many different prayers with them. Our favorite one to share, and one that my wife and I highly recommend, is the "Husband and Wife Prayer Confession." This prayer is intended for the couple to use after they are married to bring strength and unity to the relationship.

Remember that no one is perfect. When relating to serious issues, if your future mate is willing and submissive to change before the marriage, consider proceeding only if they are consistent.

* * * **Conclusion** * * *

This is just a bird's-eye view of our dominion assignment to you and others who desire "Powerful Principles for Choosing a Marriage Partner." It is my sincere hope that this book will encourage you to consider these principles before you decide to get married. Remember that no one is perfect; therefore, you will not find a perfect mate. This book is only to guide you in selecting a marriage partner as you submit to the leading of the Holy Spirit.

If you see a positive future with a special person, do not allow a negative history to damage or put a damper on your future. If your future mate is willing and submissive to change before the marriage, consider proceeding forward only if he or she is consistent. One key statement to remember is, if you desire the right person, then you must first be the right person. You must be what you desire.

May God give you wisdom to make wise choices and prudence when selecting a mate. Notice these words spoken by King Solomon in Proverbs 4:7— *"Wisdom is the principle thing."*

May God give you wisdom to make wise choices and prudence when selecting a mate.

This is saying that wisdom is first in rank. May you stay close to Jehovah Shammah, the God who is always there and forever present with you. May God bless you, may God keep you, may the wind of heaven always be at your back, pushing you forward to experience His peace, and may the joy of the Lord be your strength.

"For as many as received him, to them he gave power to become sons/daughters of God; even to them that believe on His name" (John 1:12).

The Prayer of Salvation

A born-again relationship with God is the key to a victorious life. Jesus laid down his life and rose again so that we can spend eternity with him in heaven. The Bible says, *"For God so loved the world, that he gave his only begotten Son, that whosoever believeth in him should not perish, but have everlasting life"* (John 3:16). It is the will of God that everyone receives eternal salvation.

In Romans 10:9, 13, the Bible says, *"If you shall confess with your mouth, the Lord Jesus, and shall believe in your heart that God has raised Jesus from the dead, you shall be saved."* Verse 13 says, *"For whosoever shall call upon the name of the Lord shall be saved."*

Jesus has given salvation, healing and countless benefits to all who call upon His name. These benefits can be yours if you receive him into your heart by praying this prayer: *"Heavenly Father, I come to you admitting that I am a sinner. Right now, I choose to turn away from sin, and I ask you to cleanse me from all unrighteousness. I believe that your Son*

"For God so loved the world,

that he gave his only begotten

Son, that whosoever

believeth in him should not

perish, but have

everlasting life"

(John 3:16).

Jesus died on the cross to take away my sins. I call upon the name of Jesus Christ to be the savior and Lord of my life. I choose to follow Him and I declare right now, that I am a born-again child of God. I am saved! In Jesus' name, amen."

Ask God to send spiritually

mature men and women into

your life to give you good,

godly counsel and to teach

you what husbands and

wives should do.

Future Spouse Confession

Father, I desire a Christian mate. I acknowledge that Your will be done in my life as I trust and rely on You. You have said that if I am willing and obedient to Your Word, You will give me the desires of my heart. It is my desire that someday I will be married to the person You have presented to me. I pray for him/her right now. Father, especially help him/her to grow in love; Your kind of love. A friend loves at all times, and I desire for my spouse to be a person who shares the same love that I have for You, someone who will be one in spirit and purpose with me.

I ask you to send spiritually mature men and women into our lives to give us good, godly counsel and to teach us how we should love each other and care for our family. Also, teach us what You expect husbands and wives to do and how we ought to behave towards each other. Show us Your Word concerning a marriage relationship and correct any wrong thinking in our lives. I pray that the eyes of my future spouse's understanding will be opened so that he/she will have complete knowledge of

Marriage is totally unselfish.

"Let each of you regard [esteem] one another as more important than himself" (Philippians 2:3).

Your will, in all spiritual wisdom and understanding. Father, I

pray that our commitment to each other will continually grow

as we draw closer to You. In Jesus' name, amen.

End an unhealthy

relationship

sooner rather than later.

Ending an Unhealthy Relationship

What happens if you want to end an unhealthy relation-ship? Many times, this can be a very difficult task. Below are some guidelines to help you with this assignment.

1. Pray and ask God to give you wisdom. He has promised to do that (James 1:5).

2. End the relationship as soon as possible. If you are not sure you want to marry this person, end the relationship before getting more deeply involved (Ecclesiastes 7:8).

3. Stay apart for a while to let your emotions cool down. Stay closely connected with your church family and the Word of God for empowerment (Ephesians 3:20).

4. Often, breaking up with a person may be the best favor you ever did for him/her and for yourself, especially if the relationship is unproductive (Hebrews 12:1).

5. If you need words to use, try these, "I have thought about this a long time. I do not see any future in our relationship. Please do not call or write me" (Read Proverbs 15:23).

"Get wisdom, get understanding. Wisdom is the principal thing" (Proverbs 4:7).

6. If the other person begs you to stay in the relationship and promises to change, make it a matter of prayer (Proverbs 3:6). Use wisdom and discretion over a period of time to see if the change is real (Proverbs 4:7).

7. If you are breaking up with someone who is unstable, you may need to seek emotional and spiritual help from a pastor, mature family members and friends, or a mature Christian (See Psalms 34:17).

8. In case of violence, contact your parents, pastor, or the local police for information, help, and protection (Psalms 121:1–2).

Positive Qualities

for a Great Relationship

Below is a list of positive qualities that contribute to building a great relationship. How many do you see in yourself? How many do you see in your future mate?

Admirable	Friendly	Positive
Balanced	Fun to be with	Respectful
Caring	Generous	Responsible
Committed	Gentle	Sensitive
Communicates well	Has Integrity	Shows love
Disciplined	Honest	Sincere
Empathetic	Kind	Supportive
Encourager	Listens well	Tenderhearted
Faithful	Loyal	Thoughtful
Flexible	Patient	Tolerant
Forgiving	Polite	Trustworthy

* * * About the Author * * *

Pastor Jesse L. McNeil has been a licensed minister of the Gospel for over thirty years, and has been an ordained elder for more than nineteen years. He is a graduate of the Berean Bible College of the Assemblies of God and has completed Bible courses from the Institute for Practical Ministry (with emphasis on church leadership and spiritual authority). Pastor McNeil attended the Narramore Christian Counseling School in Rosemead, California and is a Disaster Relief Advisor at Lakeland Regional Medical Center, Lakeland, Florida. With a love for children and youth, he and his wife Brenda pastored children for more than eighteen years. He also has a background in electronics and is an appliance and A/C technician.

In his local church, Pastor McNeil is actively involved as assistant pastor over the Marriage and Family Ministries, along with his wife, offering premarital and post-marital advisory to couples, as well as personal advisory. He and his wife also host a weekly radio broadcast called *Family Focus* and have worked in the community for many years, teaching marriage and family values. Pastor McNeil and his wife Brenda have

been married for more than thirty-four years. They have three

lovely children and four beautiful grandchildren.

* * * Recommended Resources * * *

- *The Successful Family* by Dr. Creflo and Taffi Dollar

- *Marriage and the Family* by Dr. Frederick K.C. Price

- *Lists to Live By for Every Married Couple*, compiled by Alice Gray, Steve Stephens, and John Van Diest

- *The Purpose and Power of Men* by Dr. Myles Monroe

- *The Purpose and Power of Woman* by Dr. Myles Monroe

- *Why You Act the Way You Do* by Tim LaHaye

- *Personality Plus* by Florence Lattauer

- *Every Teenager's Little Black Book on Sex and Dating* by Blaine Bartel

- *The Ten Commandments of Dating* by Ben Young and Samuel Adams

- *Power Ideas for a Happy Family* by Robert H. Schuller

- *Love: Fulfilling the Ultimate Quest* by James P. Gills, MD

- *The Excellent Wife* by Martha Peace

- *The Husband Handbook* by Bob Moorehead

- *So You Think You're in Love* by Greg Powe

Made in the USA
Charleston, SC
31 January 2010